Bush Theatre

T0353527

And The Rest of Me Floats

by Outbox Theatre

20 Feb – 16 Mar 2019
Bush Theatre, London

Cast

Josh-Susan Enright
Barry Fitzgerald
Elijah W Harris
Emily Joh Miller
Tamir Amar Pettet
Michelle Tiwo
Yasmin Zadeh

Creative Team

Concept and Direction	**Ben Buratta**
Producer	**Soph Nurse**
Lighting Designer	**Jess Bernberg**
Engagement Producer	**Charlotte Boden**
Voice Coach	**Susan Bovell**
Musical Director	**Neil Carter**
Stage Manager	**E Howe**
Designer	**Rūta Irbīte**
Sound Design & Original Music	**Dominic Kennedy**
Movement Director	**Coral Messam**
Production Manager	**Marco Savo**

Cast

Josh-Susan Enright

Josh-Susan is an actor, dancer and performance artist. With Outbox Josh-Susan has performed in *Affection* (The Glory); *The Front Room* (Drill Hall) and *SSA* (Central). Other credits include: *The Squash* (Tate Britain); *Pray your wings will carry you* (Full Disclosure); *Where The Lines Are Drawn* (Little Fish); *Dancer* (The Glory NT River Stage).

Barry Fitzgerald

Barry is a performer, theatre-maker and an Associate Artist of Outbox. With Outbox, Barry has performed in *Affection* (The Glory); *HOOKUP* (Hackney Showroom); *You Could Move* (Arcola); *Reach Out and Touch Me* (Shoreditch Town Hall). Other credits include: *A New Order* (BAC/The Yard); *The Lost Lending Library* (Punchdrunk); *Cleaveden Road* (Marlborough Theatre); *Belfast Boy* (Etcetera Theatre); *The Meeting* (Pleasance Theatre). As a theatre-maker and facilitator Barry has worked with the Almeida Theatre, Arcola Theatre, Gendered Intelligence, Hackney Shed, Royal Court and Unicorn Theatre.

Elijah W Harris

Elijah is an actor and writer working in film and theatre. Elijah's credits include: *The Butch Monologues* (Birmingham Rep/Soho Theatre/WoW Festival); *Brand New Boy* (Contact Manchester/Marlborough Theatre); *Corpus Christi* (Arcola); *Affection* (The Glory); *Hotel Bastille* (Camden People's Theatre); *The Poetry We Make* (RADA Festival/The Old Red Lion); *Rituals in Romance* (Spill Festival). He has also appeared in three award winning short films including: *Bleach* (dir. Jesse Lewis-Reece) and *Dusk* (dir. Jake Graf).

Elijah is currently writing a feature with Tallulah Haddon and Delaval Film, as well as working on a series for TV with co-writer Yasmin Zadeh. Elijah is a writer for Dazed Beauty and regular contributor to Ladybeard Magazine.

Emily Joh Miller

Emily is a queer actress, theatre-maker and musician. In addition to her work with Outbox she has performed in *Humanequin* (Mess Up the Mess/Wales Millenium Centre); *Galatea* (None of Us is Yet a Robot/University of Roehampton/Shakespeare Institute/The Kit) and contributed to a site-specific performance piece about the dangers of trans bathroom laws (V&A Museum). She has also carried out R&D work on various projects including: *Angels* (She's Diverse); *GRC* (Things For Your Eyes To Look At); *Orlando* (Clay & Diamonds). In addition to her work in theatre she trains and performs as a pro wrestler with women's wrestling collective Burning Hearts.

Tamir Amar Pettet

Tamir is a performer, writer and visual artist. They recently graduated from Goldsmith's with a degree in anthropology and visual practice. Their credits include: *Late Night Library Club - The Line of Beauty, Campervan Society Club* (Orange Shade Productions); *Antigone* (R&D Young Vic); *They Sat There and Talked* (Arcola Queer Collective); *Pope Joan, S'warm* (NYT). Film credits include *Milky's Immortality* (Babymorroccotv). Their written work includes Nuclear Generation and their visual artwork has been included in FRUITCAKE magazine and as part of Deptford X Fringe Festival.

Michelle Tiwo

Michelle is an actor, poet, poet educator and founder of Sistren podcast. Michelle's work is reflective of their identity and her/their communities, Nigeria & Togo via South East London. Michelle also runs poetry workshops for young people that incorporate drama and game exercises to aide in performing and storytelling. Previous collaborations and work includes: Barbican x Boy Blue, Ackee and Saltfish (BBC3), BFI x Galdem, Channel 4 Random Acts, Eastside Education x Armed Forces Service Children, Lemonade Money Productions, The Royal College of Art, Writerz n Scribez.

Yasmin Zadeh

Yasmin is a British/Iranian performer and writer. Recent credits include: *Skate Hard, Turn Left* (BAC); *HOOKUP* (Contact Manchester); *Adam and Eva* (Players Theatre, Dublin & Theatre 167, New York); *Vouchsafe* (Soho Theatre); *Big Smother* (Oval House); *Much Ado About Nothing* (Portsmouth Theatre Royal). Writing credits include: *Off.* (Arcola Theatre); *Cleavedon Road* (Marlborough Theatre); *Adam and Eva*. Yasmin has also worked with *MUJU* (The Tricycle), is an associate artist of Outbox Theatre and is currently working on a new TV series about trans identity with co-writer Elijah W Harris.

Creative Team

Ben Buratta Concept And Direction

Ben is founder and artistic director of Outbox. For Outbox, his directing credits include: *Affection* (The Glory); *HOOKUP* (Hackney Showroom/Contact); *You Could Move* (Arcola/Contact); *Reach Out and Touch Me* (Shoreditch Town Hall) and *The Front Room* (Drill Hall/mac) and curated and produced *Outbox Snapshots* (Arcola). Other credits include: *Rocket Girl* (Minack Theatre); *Quirks* (Southwark Playhouse); *Tasty* (Arcola) and a wide range of projects and productions for communities across the UK. He regularly collaborates with queer artists and theatre-makers to offer creative support.

Ben is a lecturer and director at Royal Central School of Speech and Drama where he is currently undertaking a practice-based PhD in creating rehearsal strategies and dramaturgies for queer performance.

Soph Nurse Producer

Soph is an independent producer whose experience includes work at Bush Theatre, Royal Court and Forced Entertainment. Theatre credits include: *Skate Hard, Turn Left* (BAC); *DIGS* (CPT, Pleasance, Pleasance Courtyard); *The Last Straw* (Ovalhouse); *People Show: 50th Year* (Toynbee Studios); *Give Me Your Skin* (BAC, Marlborough, Bike Shed), *BABY/LON* (Hackney Showroom).

Rūta Irbīte Designer

Rūta is a London based freelance designer for performance. She trained in Performance Design and Practice at Central Saint Martin's College of Art and Design, graduating with a first class diploma in 2013. She was a shortlisted finalist for the Linbury Prize for Stage Design 2013.

Her recent public theatre design work include: *SLIME* (Hull City Libraries); *A New Order* (The Yard/Live Drafts); *And The Rest of Me Floats* (Rose Lipman/Birmingham Rep); *Girl Meets Boy* (The Yard/First Drafts); *Sea Fret* (Old Red Lion); *Open Court* (Royal Court); *Mumburger* (The Archivist's Gallery); *The Session* (Soho Upstairs); *Primetime* (Royal Court).

Rūta is a returning visiting professional at Central School of Speech and Drama where she works with Drama, Applied Theatre and Education students to create designs for their devised pieces. She is associate designer for The Herd Theatre and has repeatedly worked with Outbox Theatre and inclusive theatre companies Blink Dance Theatre and Face Front.

Coral Messam Movement Director

Coral is a performer and movement director who works across theatre, television and film. Recent movement director/choreographer credits include: *Britannia – Season 2* (Sky Atlantic); *Humans* (Channel 4); *Game of Thrones* (HBO); *The Winter's Tale* (Globe); *Fantastic Follies of Mrs Rich* (RSC); *One Love: The Bob Marley Musical* (Birmingham Rep); *Macbeth* (Globe); *King Lear* (Royal Exchange); *Ma Rainey's Black Bottom* (NT). Director debut: *Run it Back* (Talawa/Hackney Showroom).

Dominic Kennedy Sound Designer

Dominic is a Sound Designer, Composer and Music Producer who has a keen interest in developing new work and implementing sound and music at an early stage in a creative process. Dominic is a graduate from Royal Central School of Speech and Drama where he developed specialist skills in collaborative and devised theatre making, music composition and installation practices. His work often fuses found sound, field recordings, music composition and synthesis. Recent credits include: *Skate Hard, Turn Left* (BAC); *Roundabout Season 2018, Roundabout Season 2017, Broken Biscuits, Roundabout Season 2016, With A Little Bit Of Luck, The Human Ear* (Paines Plough); *The Assassination of Katie Hopkins* (Theatre Clywd); *Ramona Tells Jim* (Bush Theatre); *I am a Tree* (Jamie Wood); *Box Clever* (nabokov); *Gap In The Light, Run* (Engineer), *The Devil Speaks True* (Goat and Monkey); *ONO* (Jamie Wood).

Jess Bernberg Lighting Designer

Jess is a graduate of Guildhall School of Music and Drama and the 2018 Laboratory Associate Lighting Designer at Nuffield Southampton Theatres. She received the Association of Lighting Designer's Francis Reid Award in 2017.

Design credits include: *Medusa, Much Ado About Nothing, Dungeness, Love and Information* (Nuffield Southampton Theatres); *Fabric, Drip Feed* (Soho Theatre); *Homos, or Everyone in America* (Finborough Theatre); *SongLines* (HighTide); *A New and Better You, Buggy Baby* (The Yard); *The Marbleous Route Home* (Young Vic); *Reactor* (Arts Ed); *Devil with the Blue Dress, FCUK'D* - Off West End Award nomination (The Bunker); *Split, WAYWARD* (Vaults); *Ajax* (The Space); *The Blue Hour of Natalie Barney, The Dowager's Oyster, Youkali: The Pursuit of Happiness, The Selfish Giant* (Arcola Theatre); *The Death of Ivan Ilyich* (Merton Arts Space); *And the Rest of Me Floats* (Birmingham Rep); *And Here I Am* (UK Tour. Co-Design with Andy Purves); *The Poetry We Make* (Vaults Festival/RADA/Rosemary Branch/Old Red Lion); *This is Matty, and He is Fucked* (Winemaker's Club); *Flux: Shadowlines* (King's Place); *SQUIRM* (King's Head/Theatre503/Bread & Roses Theatre/C Venues);

Glitter & Tears (Bread & Roses Theatre/theSpace UK); *Balm in Gilead, The Same Deep Water As Me, August* (Guildhall). As Assistant Lighting Designer: *A Streetcar Named Desire* (Nuffield Southampton Theatres); *A Tale of Two Cities* (Regent's Park Open Air Theatre); *A Fox on the Fairway* (Queen's Theatre Hornchurch).

Neil Carter Musical Director

Neil trained at Rose Bruford College of Speech and Drama as an Actor-Musician. Theatre credits include: *Threepenny* (Opera Theatr Clwyd); *Little Shop Of Horrors* (Haymarket Basingstoke); *Mary and The Shaman* (BAC); *Mother Makes Three* (Oldham Colosseum); *Happy End* (National Tour). He has written music for TV and Film including The Muppets Most Wanted which he considers his best and most ridiculous work. He went on to be an Associate at the National Theatre and Drama consultant at the Barbican before founding The Primary Shakespeare Company, an Arts Educational Charity working with mainstream and specials schools across London.

Charlotte Boden Engagement Producer

Charlotte is co-founder and co-director of The Queer House, an artists agency and production house for LGBTQIA+ actors and makers. Charlotte currently produces for Annie Siddons and Mia Johnson. Theatre credits include: *Pink Lemonade* (CPT, Curve, Derby Theatre, Nottingham Playhouse), *And The Rest of Me Floats* (Rose Lipman, Birmingham Rep).

About Outbox Theatre

Outbox make theatre queerly.

We collaborate with LGBTQ+ performers, artists and communities to tell stories in bold and exciting ways.

Our theatre moves; we are playful with form, taking inspiration from (and blurring the lines of) performance, dance and visual art.

Though often found in unusual spaces and buildings, we also collaborate with leading theatres and arts organisations including Birmingham REP, Leeds Playhouse, Bristol Old Vic, The Royal Court and the Bush.

Outbox was founded in 2010 by Artistic Director, Ben Buratta, with a mission to tell the unheard and forgotten stories of the queer community, our work is inter-generational and inclusive.

At Outbox our participation work sits proudly alongside our creative programme; one cannot exist without the other. We want to share what we create, pass on any skills we learn along the way and keep learning from the LGBTQ+ community.

We work with LGBTQ+ youth groups nationally to build skills in performance, confidence building and self-esteem. We connect with older LGBTQ+ people too – visiting social groups, residential homes and working with charities such as Age UK. Our goal is always to bring different sections of the LGBTQ+ community together, across generations and cultures, to create a dialogue and an exciting shared experience.

Outbox are supported by Royal Central School of Speech and Drama, Big Lottery Fund and Arts Council England.

We want our audiences to challenge, question and, ultimately, dance with us… We are never far away from a mirror-ball, a smoke machine, and a glitter-drop.

Thank You's

Big thanks go to the following individuals and organisations for making the show possible:

Madani Younis, Lise Bell and Stewart Pringle for believing in our show and championing it.

The Bush Team.

Professor Maria Delgado, Dan Hetherington, Sally Baggott, and the Research Department at Royal Central School of Speech and Drama.

Our amazing partner The Queer House and BOiBOX for bringing all the fun for BOiBUSH.

Gendered Intelligence. Mark Powell and Prime Theatre. Steve Ball and Birmingham REP.

Stephen Farrier. David Harradine. Jodi Gray. Jemima James. Nike Jonah. Sheena Khanna. Kayza Rose. Andrew Ellerby. Amber Evans. Kieran Salt. Saskia Grundmann.

Serena Grasso and Oberon Books.

All the queer people who have taken part in our workshops, performed in our shows and supported our work. We salute you.

Bush Theatre

Bush
Theatre
We make theatre
for London. Now.

The Bush is a world-famous home for new plays
and an internationally renowned champion of
playwrights. We discover, nurture and produce
the best new writers from the widest range of
backgrounds from our home in a distinctive corner
of west London.

The Bush has won over 100 awards and developed
an enviable reputation for touring its acclaimed
productions nationally and internationally.

We are excited by exceptional new voices,
stories and perspectives – particularly those with
contemporary bite which reflect the vibrancy of
British culture now.

Located in the newly renovated old library on
Uxbridge Road in the heart of Shepherd's Bush,
the theatre houses two performance spaces, a
rehearsal room and the lively Library Bar.

 Supported by
ARTS COUNCIL
ENGLAND

 h&f
hammersmith & fulham

bushtheatre.co.uk

THANK YOU

The Bush Theatre would like to thank all its supporters whose valuable contributions have helped us to create a platform for our future and to promote the highest quality new writing, develop the next generation of creative talent, lead innovative community engagement work and champion diversity.

LONE STAR
Gianni Alen-Buckley
Michael Alen-Buckley
Rafael & Anne-Helene Biosse Duplan
Garvin & Steffanie Brown
Alice Findlay
Charles Holloway
Miles Morland

HANDFUL OF STARS
Dawn & Gary Baker
Charlie Bigham
Judy Bollinger
Clive & Helena Butler
Grace Chan
Clare & Chris Clark
Clyde Cooper
Sue Fletcher
Richard & Jane Gordon
Priscilla John
Simon & Katherine Johnson
Philippa Seal & Philip Jones QC
Joanna Kennedy
V&F Lukey
Robert Ledger & Sally Mousdale
Georgia Oetker
Philip & Biddy Percival
Clare Rich
Joana & Henrik Schliemann
Lesley Hill & Russ Shaw
van Tulleken Family
and one anonymous donor.

RISING STARS
ACT IV
Nicholas Alt
Mark Bentley
David Brooks
Catharine Browne
Matthew Byam Shaw
Tim & Andrea Clark
Sarah Clarke
Claude & Susie Cochin de Billy
Lois Cox
Susie Cuff
Matthew Cushen
Philippa Dolphin
John Fraser
Jack Gordon & Kate Lacy
Hugh & Sarah Grootenhuis
Jessica Ground
Thea Guest
Patrick Harrison
Ann & Ravi Joseph
Davina & Malcolm Judelson
Miggy Littlejohns

RISING STARS (continued)
Isabella Macpherson
Liz & Luke Mayhew
Michael McCoy
Judith Mellor
Caro Millington
Dan & Laurie Mucha
Mark & Anne Paterson
Pippa Prain
Barbara Prideaux
Emily Reeve
Renske & Marion
Sarah Richards
Julian Riddick
Susie Saville Sneath
Saleem & Alexandra Siddiqi
Brian Smith
Peter Tausig
Guy Vincent & Sarah Mitchell
Trish Wadley
Amanda Waggott
Alison Winter
and three anonymous donors.

SPONSORS & SUPPORTERS
AKA
Alen-Buckley LLP
Gianni & Michael Alen-Buckley
Jeremy Attard Manche
Bill & Judy Bollinger
Edward Bonham Carter
Martin Bowley
Duke & Duchess of Buccleuch
The Hon Mrs Louise Burness
Sir Charles & Lady Isabella Burrell
Philip & Tita Byrne
CHK Charities Limited
Peppe & Quentin Ciardi
Joanna & Hadyn Cunningham
Leo & Grega Daly
Patrick & Mairead Flaherty
Sue Fletcher
The Hon Sir Rocco Forte
The Hon Portia Forte
Mark Franklin
The Gatsby Charitable Foundation
The Right Hon Piers Gibson
Farid & Emilie Gragour
Victoria Gray
John Gordon
Vivienne Guinness
Melanie Hall
The Headley Trust
Brian Heyworth
Lesley Hill & Russ Shaw

SPONSORS & SUPPORTERS (continued)
Michael Holland & Denise O'Donoghue
Charles Holloway
Graham & Amanda Hutton
James Gorst Architects Ltd.
Simon & Katherine Johnson
Tarek & Diala Khlat
Bernard Lambilliotte
Marion Lloyd
The Lord Forte Foundation
Peter & Bettina Mallinson
Mahoro Charitable Trust
James Christopher Miller
Mitsui Fodosan (U.K.) Ltd
Alfred Munkenbeck III
Nick Hern Books
Georgia Oetker
RAB Capital
Kevin Pakenham
Sir Howard Panter
Joanna Prior
Josie Rourke
Lady Susie Sainsbury
Barry Serjent
Tim & Catherine Score
Search Foundation
Richard Sharp
Susie Simkins
Edward Snape & Marilyn Eardley
Michael & Sarah Spencer
Stanhope PLC
Ross Turner
The Syder Foundation
van Tulleken Family
Johnny & Dione Verulam
Robert & Felicity Waley-Cohen
Elizabeth Wigoder
Phillip Wooller
Danny Wyler
and three anonymous donors.

TRUSTS AND FOUNDATIONS
The Andrew Lloyd Webber Foundation
The Boris Karloff Foundation
The Boshier-Hinton Foundation
The Bruce Wake Charitable Trust
The Chapman Charitable Trust
The City Bridge Trust
Cockayne—Grants for the Arts
The John S Cohen Foundation
The Daisy Trust
The Equity Charitable Trust
Esmée Fairbairn Foundation
Fidelio Charitable Trust

TRUSTS AND FOUNDATIONS (continued)
Foyle Foundation
Garfield Weston Foundation
Garrick Charitable Trust
Hammersmith United Charities
Heritage of London Trust
John Lyon's Charity
The J Paul Getty Jnr Charitable Trust
The John Thaw Foundation
The Kirsten Scott Memorial Trust
The Leverhulme Trust
The London Community Foundation
The Martin Bowley Charitable Trust
The Monument Trust
The Noel Coward Foundation
Paul Hamlyn Foundation
Peter Wolff Foundation
Pilgrim Trust
The Royal Victoria Hall Foundation
Sir John Cass's Foundation
Stavros Niarchos Foundation
The Theatres Trust
Viridor Credits
The Williams Charitable Trust
Western Riverside Worshipful Company of Mercers Environmental Fund
The Wolfson Foundation
and one anonymous donor.

CORPORATE SPONSORS AND MEMBERS
The Agency (London) Ltd
Dorsett Shepherds Bush
Drama Centre London
Fever Tree
The Groucho Club
THE HOXTON
Philip Wooller
Westfield London

PUBLIC FUNDING

If you are interested in finding out how to be involved, please visit **bushtheatre.co.uk/support-us** or email **development@bushtheatre.co.uk** or call **020 8743 3584**.

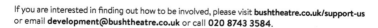

AND THE REST OF ME FLOATS

Outbox Theatre

AND THE REST OF ME FLOATS

OBERON BOOKS
LONDON

WWW.OBERONBOOKS.COM

First published in 2019 by Oberon Books Ltd
521 Caledonian Road, London N7 9RH
Tel: +44 (0) 20 7607 3637 / Fax: +44 (0) 20 7607 3629
e-mail: info@oberonbooks.com
www.oberonbooks.com

PB ISBN: 9781786827296
E ISBN: 9781786827333

Cover design by Studio Doug
Cover photography by Bronwen Sharp

eBook conversion by Lapiz Digital Services, India.

10 9 8 7 6 5 4 3 2 1

A Note on the Play

*A*nd *The Rest of Me Floats* is a play about the messiness of gender, and the text, imagery, movement, and form reflect the themes of the show. As a company, we began the devising process in 2017 with Josh-Susan, Barry, Elijah, Emily, Tamir, Miiko and Yasmin. The show was then programmed by the Bush for their 2019 season and, as Miiko was not available, Michelle joined the company. As the play is built around the performers' identity and relationship to their gender this made big changes to the script and the process.

The play is form-busting; swerving realism means that the linear, causal narratives that see trans and queer people victimised, in trauma and in danger could be re-authored by the performers. Playing with form allowed for alternative and autonomous ways for performers to share their biographies, gender expressions and identities. Rehearsals would often begin with dressing up, karaoke, lip-synching and stand-up and one morning on the first week of the rehearsal process, Elijah was performing some jokes around his identity:

> ELIJAH: When rehearsing for a play and the director
>   says let's try that transition again, you say
>   'Again?!'

Elijah's joke around transition – as well as really making us all laugh – became a pivotal moment in the making process. He usefully and poignantly riffed on the meaning of transition. This struck me both in terms of gender confirmation and the dramaturgical meaning of a transition. In a normative process, the transition in theatre acts as the connective tissue between scenes, it is clearly defined and takes us from one section of a play to the next. Elijah's joke allowed us to consider the theatrical transition in a different way, and ask of it: what happens when the transition becomes central to the rehearsal process? Can the scenes in a play interrupt the transition?

The orchestration and queering of time also played into the work we made; in one rehearsal exercise all actors and creative team were asked to write a timeline of events in their lives. The lists were to be factual and chronological. Certain moments, places and events chimed; multiple and varied coming-outs, gender identity clinics, names and pronouns, love and sex, friendships, music, TV and cinema. However, the company were struck with the coherence and the order of the lists; the lines and formality of the biographies didn't match the messiness of the experiences lived. This is reflected in the play text; the numbers appear in patterns across the page and emerge and subsequently disappear throughout the piece.

Alongside the numbers, facts and figures, are questions which hang in the air, spoken but never answered. The supple plasticity of the transition harnessed the shifting form of the stories being told until, near the end of the play, the transition is completely ruptured.

Most importantly, the company wanted to make a piece that celebrates gender diversity, in all its glory. We hope that when you are reading the play or performing the text you experience the same joy we felt creating it. Don't be afraid to change the order, re-write the text, and break the rules.

Ben Buratta

And The Rest of Me Floats was originally performed at Rose Lipman Building, London and Birmingham REP (as part of SHOUT festival) in 2017. Supported by Big Lottery Fund. Cast and creatives from the original production were as follows:

Cast	Josh-Susan Enright
	Barry Fitzgerald
	Elijah W Harris
	Emily Joh Miller
	Tamir Amar Pettet
	Mikko Toivianen
	Yasmin Zadeh
Concept and Direction	Ben Buratta
Assistant Director	Griffyn Gilligan
Producer	Charlotte Boden
Production Manager	James Asquith
Lighting Designer	Jess Bernberg
Voice Coach	Susan Bovell
Musical Director	Neil Carter
Graphic Designer	Brenda Fitzgerald
Stage Manager	E Howe
Designer	Rūta Irbīte
Sound Design & Original Music	Dominic Kennedy
Movement Director	Coral Messam

And The Rest of Me Floats was revived at the Bush Theatre, London in February 2019. Supported by Arts Council England, Royal Central School of Speech and Drama, and Prime Theatre. Cast and creatives for the revived production were as follows:

Cast	Josh-Susan Enright
	Barry Fitzgerald
	Elijah W Harris
	Emily Joh Miller
	Tamir Amar Pettet
	Michelle Tiwo
	Yasmin Zadeh
Concept and Direction	Ben Buratta
Producer	Soph Nurse
Lighting Designer	Jess Bernberg
Engagement Producer	Charlotte Boden
Voice Coach	Susan Bovell
Musical Director	Neil Carter
Stage Manager	E Howe
Designer	Rūta Irbīte
Sound Design & Original Music	Dominic Kennedy
Movement Director	Coral Messam
Production Manager	Marco Savo

Notes:

All text in **bold** is delivered through microphones

Timelines take place at the edge of the stage and numbers are spoken by actors to indicate their various ages

/ indicates an overlap in speech

A break in the text indicates a pause/space in time

There are no 'characters' as such. Performers tell their own stories, wear their own clothes and speak in their own accents

– indicates that the actor is saying lines that don't represent who they are

All 'scenes' have been given titles

This edition of the play text reflects the show as it was performed at the Bush Theatre, February 2019.

The performers arrive individually. They come into the space and 'meet' the audience; making direct eye contact, allowing the audience to really take them in. This goes on for an almost uncomfortable amount of time.

TIMELINE 1

35

34

6

5

ELIJAH: nightmares about fire begin

21

TAMIR: come out as non-binary

2   4

7   3   21

18

EMILY: Finally, start taking hormones.

15   3   4

27

JOSH-SUSAN: Colour

27

ELIJAH: And the rest of me floats

11

GRID

*The company perform a tightly choreographed grid-like sequence;
BARRY, ELIJAH and MICHELLE perform one route, JOSH-SUSAN and
EMILY perform the second, and TAMIR and YASMIN perform the third.
There are beats playing based on 80s New York house. Their walks
are exaggerated versions of each other's gait. They plod, mince, stomp,
stride, glide and sashay through the sequence, constrained by the strict
pathways created for them.*

THE INTERNET

– **Our baby is talking to strangers**

– **He is lonely**

– **They don't seem to have many friends**

– **They need to spend some time with real
  people**

TAMIR: Gender is performative

           they said

           or is that me

           they

           or them

           distant from knowing or showing

           performing an alluring version of myself

12

I was born in 1994, then came Windows 95,
and I would dive online,

on *Habbo Hotel* to be the true me,

a two-cm avatar with a denim mini and a
high pony.

Online, all the time, to avoid conversation
and the frustration of being a He, which
wasn't me, or her

TAMIR/YASMIN:	Can you see me?
TAMIR:	Oh, sorry my cam's broke/
YASMIN:	My camera doesn't work sometimes.
T/Y:	Are you there?
TAMIR:	I love Dairy Milk chocolate
YASMIN:	I'm a music producer, a record producer. No, wait, I work in the music industry
TAMIR:	I'm Gemma Genocide, scene queen, ruled by the darkness
YASMIN:	Calvin, but you can call me Cal, everyone does
TAMIR:	I bet you say that to all the girls/
YASMIN:	Do you talk to other guys

TAMIR:	How would you kiss me?
YASMIN:	I'm working on a track for Stormzy
T/Y:	What are you up to right now?
TAMIR:	I live in town
YASMIN:	LA is cool, but Southampton is more chill.
T/Y:	Can you see me?
TAMIR:	So annoying my camera is fucked/
YASMIN:	I'll have to pick up another from the studio
TAMIR:	Can we cam tomorrow
YASMIN:	I'll sort it for tomorrow
TAMIR:	My band is doing really well at the moment, we are called My Screaming Heart
YASMIN:	I used to have a girlfriend but she got too clingy. I'm single at the moment.
TAMIR:	I wrote a song called 'This girl won't bleed again', it's not out yet
YASMIN:	Bacardi and Coke
TAMIR:	Absinthe straight up, sometimes with Coke.
YASMIN:	Do you want to meet me?
TAMIR:	We should meet

TAMIR: I felt free in cyberspace

                that way I couldn't face the physicality of
                prickly hairs,

                of being a MAN who is a he,

                not me, them or he?

                Or she, get back to the digital it's never
                critical of your brilliant femininity,

                where I could exist freely,

                as a he, who was a she, who felt like a he
                sometimes or a she at others,

                or completely they,

                I say, you say, but it doesn't feel the same.

–   **It's dangerous**

–   **Maybe they are being groomed**

–   **Catfished**

–   **Who are they talking to?**

YASMIN: Describe your perfect date

TAMIR: Are you flirting with me

YASMIN:	He sounds like a dick, I wouldn't do that to you
TAMIR:	Most guys are intimidated by me.
YASMIN:	I would fly you to New York and I would probably take you to this club I know. We don't have to do anything. Just get to know each other. I'm not like that.
TAMIR:	I think it's because I am funnier than them.
YASMIN:	I wear gold chains
TAMIR:	Red hair extensions
YASMIN:	I used to have a beard but at the moment it's just stubble
TAMIR:	I always wear purple knickers
YASMIN:	People say I look like Justin Timberlake.
TAMIR:	Heels, never flats.
YASMIN:	I wish you could see me
TAMIR:	I could talk to you all day
YASMIN:	Do you wanna go out with me?
TAMIR:	We talk a lot.
YASMIN:	I feel really trapped sometimes
TAMIR:	I hate school I just want to get out

YASMIN:	When I talk to people sometimes they don't listen
TAMIR:	They wouldn't understand
YASMIN:	Hey…?
TAMIR:	Hello?
TAMIR:	Back surfing the web

on its temperamental wave

I wave goodbye to my physicality he, she,
they and me,

and liberated by freedom of the internet for
it knows me digitally, not through language
but through binary code

I'm not in a binary mode

I am limitless

TEENAGE DIRTBAG

ELIJAH sings 'Teenage Dirtbag' by Wheatus, backed by the cast on piano and drums. The song begins slowly, we don't know what it is to begin with, and then it all kicks off into a teenage rock star fantasy.

TIMELINE 2

27

> **3**

> **15**

24

7   **14**

18

EMILY: **Citizens of Facebook, I am a woman.
                  My name is Emily.**

7

BARRY: **Mary Barry. The big girl's blouse**

5

YASMIN: **Clarissa explains it all**

17

MICHELLE: **Played Michael in the Church play**

                  10

YASMIN: **I am Max**

14

MICHELLE: **Get my first chin hair**

PLASTIC DUET

A sheet of plastic is held by BARRY and YASMIN and is wrapped around, by and through ELIJAH and TAMIR. On the mics, MICHELLE, JOSH-SUSAN and EMILY speak the questions that they are often asked, such as:

EMILY: How long have you known?

              Have you always wanted to be an actor?

              Do you have to label yourself like that?

              Aren't we all just people?

              How many surgeries have you had?

              How did you choose your name?

              Are you American?

              Do you want to do anything tonight?

              Are you okay with this?

              Do we need to make things so political?

              Do you have a boyfriend?

              Have you tried mindfulness?

What kinks do you have?

JOSH-SUSAN: Why are you wearing a dress?

Are you a transvestite?

Where are you actually from?

Do you like sex?

Would you want to get breasts?

Do you want a bump, a shot or a fag?

What's your heritage?

Are you offended?

Who are you?

Why did you leave?

Do you love me?

What can we do to be more
accommodating?

What's your diagnosis?

MICHELLE: How does it feel?

Is there something you wanna tell us?

Why you so passionate about gay rights?
Are you gay or something?

Why you always wearing baggy clothes?

How do lesbians even have sex?

So what, you eat pussy?

When will you marry?

Do you have any spiritual practices?

Where are you *from* from?

What does patriarchy mean?

It doesn't really count as sex though, does it?

How many sexual partners have you had?

Why d'you sound like a white girl?

Does this mean you don't like Sean Paul
anymore?

Which Hogwarts house are you in?

What kinda women are you attracted to?

You down for a threesome?

Can I set you up with someone?

What do you think of her?

Why d'you always have to be the different one?

Can't you just dress like normal girls?

Why're you wearing your Converses so tight?

Is she your type?

Do you still like dick?

Are you new here?

Why don't you show off your body more?

What's your favourite position?

Ah, you know who you remind me of?

COMING OUTS

ELIJAH: Mum… Mum, can I just talk to you about
               something, quickly?

               Yeah, I know you've got to go, it's just…

               Sometimes I fancy boys. And sometimes I
               fancy girls.

MICHELLE: Bet I would've been taller, if I were a boy.
               I woulda been sexy though, all the galdems'
               favourite sugar. Mandem woulda called
               me sweet boy to hide the fact they felt
               threatened by my confidence and charm.
               Man woulda just glided into rooms on some
               big-dick-energy shit like, 'What you saying
               babes?'

ELIJAH: Okay, I guess I just feel really unhappy in
               my body.

               Like, I can't relate to it.

MICHELLE:	Wish I coulda told someone that, though. Wish I had someone to run to and say, 'Hey I feel like a different person stuck in my own body today, do you ever feel like that?'
ELIJAH:	I can't relate to having breasts. I hate them.
MICHELLE:	Without becoming school gossip. Without becoming an alien.
ELIJAH:	I just don't feel like a girl.
MICHELLE:	It was bad enough if they found out you were gay.
ELIJAH:	Okay, I know I've done this a few times now –
MICHELLE:	Do I see myself with a woman or a man five years from now? Do I have to choose?
ELIJAH:	But, I wanted to say that I'm starting to sometimes be attracted to…
MICHELLE:	I feel like I need to be with men, though.
ELIJAH:	…male-bodied people, actually just people.
MICHELLE:	I like men.

GRANDMA

*(In our version BARRY plays Grandma and YASMIN plays a version of
ELIJAH's younger self.)*

–	I wanted you to have this…
–	This
–	Why don't you try it on
–	It's cool

ELIJAH: It's not about gender or sex anymore.

MICHELLE: /I feel sorry for anyone born even an inch
               outside of society's box of norms. Don't get
               me wrong. I don't hate my body, I just don't
               always want it, but I'm not ready to give it
               back yet. Yeah it's wild.

               I DON'T MEAN TO BE LIKE THIS

               I just feel like

               I just don't feel like

ELIJAH: /This isn't me, it's not mine. My mind floats
               and my body is stuck; you know? I suppose
               it's about positionality, I'm freer now, it's
               shifting.

               I know you're not surprised, I need this,
               I NEED something to change. I'm sorry.

I just feel like

I just don't feel like

–   It was your grandfather's

–   Yeah I know

–   It should fit you, it was his favourite

        Turn around

        Very smart, very handsome

–   I love it.

–   It's yours. Don't lose it

–   I won't. No need to nag

–   I did nag didn't I

–   All the time, it was annoying

–   Sometimes I enjoyed the nagging

–   You were silly.

–   Telling me to do things that didn't make sense

–   I don't think they made any sense to me. My mind played tricks on me

-          Dishcloths don't belong in the kettle Nana

-          I know that now, of course

-          Is there someone special?

-          Err, none of your business

-          I know there is

-          Oh then why are you asking?

-          I wanted you to tell me

-          Well maybe I don't want to

-          You can tell me

-          Maybe there is

-          Are you happy?

-          Well you seem to know everything so

-          I think you are

-          I think you're right

-          Let me see

-          You look like him you have his eyes

-          Really?

–   Really

–   More so now?

–   More so now

–   We used to go dancing. He was wearing that
         when we met.

–   I can't dance

–   Dance with me

–   You'd have to teach me

–   This way, no, this way. You can lead

–   I don't know how

–   That's it

–   I'm going to trip you up

–   Give me a twirl

–   There/

–   There

–   It's not the same here without you.

–   I miss you.

–   Do you see me?

–   I do

–   Really see me? Now.

–   Now, I couldn't before…

–   I know.

–   Very nice. It suits you.

GRID 2

The company revisit the grid from the beginning of the play. The same beats play. The grid is more fragmented now, the rigid formality of the first grid is breaking down and becoming a bit messier. EMILY is being dressed up by BARRY. She rejects and accepts the clothes, until she finds the outfit that feels most powerful for her – a fur coat and shades.

TIMELINE 3

2

1

13

MICHELLE:	**start my period it's the fucking worst**
ELIJAH:	**start my period it is hell on earth**

7   **7**

          18   **18**

YASMIN:	**Don't you just want to look nice?**
BARRY:	**Who's the girl in the relationship?**

                    18

18

18

JOSH-SUSAN:	**Head to Drama School to do Musical Theatre and am repeatedly told to 'Man Up'**

          3

               7

MEDICINE

ELIJAH:	When did you first realise that you wanted to transition?
EMILY:	How do you feel?

Does that hurt?

JOSH-SUSAN: Did you fuck him or did he fuck you?

ELIJAH: Why did you try to kill yourself?

JOSH-SUSAN: Do you take drugs?

EMILY: Take this form and fill it out.

ELIJAH: Do you think you're not good-looking
                enough?

JOSH-SUSAN: I don't really know how to answer that
                question.

EMILY: I've never *not* known.

ELIJAH: Would you say you have quite a nihilistic
                view of the world?

                Do you want to try anti-depressants?

EMILY: Are you having the kind of sex you want
                to have?

JOSH-SUSAN: You feel tethered, like a horse to a fence.

EMILY: Do you see me?

ELIJAH: Try not to cry.

EMILY: Oesclim

                Estraderm

                Oestradiol

JOSH-SUSAN:	Is *anyone* having the kind of sex they want?
EMILY:	Promethium
	Provera
	Estradot
	Estrace
ELIJAH:	Would you say your handwriting is more curved and lyrical or direct and indelicate?
EMILY:	Sorry.
	What the fuck?
JOSH-SUSAN:	Should you be on medication?
	Medication alone is not the answer.
ELIJAH:	I need to cry
	Try not to cry.
JOSH-SUSAN:	Do you see me?
ELIJAH:	If your genitals were crushed in some kind of accident…
EMILY:	Do you think your depression may be due to the fact that you are just starting to live as a woman?
	Do you see yourself continuing to enter romantic relationships with women once you begin transitioning?

ELIJAH:	Abso-fucking-lutely
JOSH-SUSAN:	That's a relief
	Why did you try to kill yourself?
EMILY:	Dry mouth, some shaking, palpitations
ELIJAH:	Nebido
	Reandron
	Sustanon
	Jenasteron
	Primoteston
JOSH-SUSAN:	Broccoli
ELIJAH:	Broccoli?
JOSH-SUSAN:	Mmm-hmm
EMILY:	So, it looks like the hormones are working! I bet the boys are all over you.
JOSH-SUSAN:	Mmm-hmm
EMILY:	Do you feel like a girl or do you think that comes from dissatisfaction with other things in your life?
JOSH-SUSAN:	Try not to cry.
EMILY:	Lift your shirt up for me

	Is there any chance you could be pregnant?
ELIJAH:	That's very fucking unlikely
JOSH-SUSAN:	On a scale of one to ten, ten being the most…
	You would like me to refer you for a hysterectomy
	Don't worry you're not a psychopath. If you were, you wouldn't be worried about it.
EMILY:	This feels a bit invasive actually. Could we just stop
JOSH-SUSAN:	When did *you* first realise you were a boy?
	If you were acting in a play, would you want to play a male or female character?
EMILY:	Sorry, in normal circumstances, we don't prescribe oestrogen to anybody under thirty-five
JOSH-SUSAN:	I see you're wearing a T-shirt and jeans. Did you know you don't have to be male or female?
ELIJAH:	Were you better at maths or English?
	Are you more creative or scientific?
EMILY:	Do you see me?
ELIJAH:	The local funding group won't cover anything cosmetic.

JOSH-SUSAN: Now you will feel a short, sharp scratch

100 WAYS

MICHELLE sings '100 Ways To Be A Good Girl' by Skunk Anansie.
It is bluesy and raw – backing by BARRY on piano, EMILY on guitar
and ELIJAH on drums.

FINDING THE LIGHT

Darkness. The cast dress and undress, discovered and revealed by the
light of MICHELLE's torch. They exchange different items of clothing.
The torch alternatively searches, objectifies, interrogates, and illuminates.
The performers begin to confront the light, they begin to walk into the
audience, until the light finds JOSH-SUSAN…

DO YOU SEE ME

JOSH-SUSAN: Do you see me?

                I mean, beyond the fabulous figure-hugging
                frock and the mismatched baritone tone

                Do you really see me?

                You and your mates want a selfie but you're
                not really looking at me. Your eyes buzz all
                around my body – the dots not quite joining
                up – but they don't meet me.

                You sulk when I say no, but I keep on
                dancing. I'm the kid who danced his way

out of chaos, like a brown Billy Elliot.
Except I never got to swim in Swan Lake.
Cos places like that weren't for people like
me. Or so I was told. But I kept moving.
When they told me to straighten my spine
and ground my hips, I grooved through,
around and between their pronouns. Never
quite settling for one, letting my body do
the talking.

Is my voice too deep for you? Is my body
too lithe, too dark, too effeminate? Are you
confused?

I'm a man. In a dress. That I found in a bin.
Is something funny?

I'm not gonna aggrieve you. I'm not going to
be the angry, inarticulate object you want me
to be. My mind floats and my body is stuck

Or is it the other way around. It feels like
'me' is deep and this is just a shell. But this
shell can still look pretty fucking pretty.
Adorned with lycra and polyester blend
but not your pity. And certainly not your
violence.

Not tonight.

Cos tonight I can be Rihanna *and* I can be
her rude boy. Both.

So why don't you bore someone else with
your questions.

RELIGION

BARRY: Bless me father for I have sinned.

It has been twenty-three years since my last confession

MICHELLE: Be an example for your siblings, they said, you're our firstborn. You need to be God-fearing, like a Proverbs 31 woman.

TAMIR: *Sh'ma Yisra'eil Adonai Eloheinu Adonai echad.*

–   **Repeat**

TAMIR: *Sh'ma Yisra'eil Adonai Eloheinu Adonai echad.*

–   **Repeat**

TAMIR: *Sh'ma Yisra'eil Adonai Eloheinu Adonai echad.*

YASMIN: Who is in that picture on the wall?

MICHELLE: How come God's a man?

YASMIN: Why do we speak another language at home?

MICHELLE: Couldn't he be a woman?

YASMIN: Does Maman Bouzorg like me?

MICHELLE: But I thought God was everything?

YASMIN: Why can't we eat at the table like ordinary people?

MICHELLE: Are gay people really going to hell?

YASMIN: Is all music written in Farsi?

MICHELLE: Every Sunday – Sunday best, praise the Lord, home for jollof and chicken, then school mass on Wednesdays and Fridays, church again on Sunday

YASMIN: We buy a lamb from Macro and eat it Sunday, Monday, Tuesday, Wednesday, Thursday, Friday and buy another lamb on Saturday.

TAMIR: *Sh'ma Yisra'eil Adonai Eloheinu Adonai echad.*

– **Repeat**

TAMIR: *Sh'ma Yisra'eil Adonai Eloheinu Adonai echad.*

– **Repeat**

TAMIR: *Sh'ma Yisra'eil Adonai Eloheinu Adonai echad.*

– **Repeat**

BARRY: I didn't set the table when Mammy asked me.

37

I convinced my older brother he was adopted.

I wore my sister's Communion dress.

I'm not like my brothers.

I wondered why girls get all the clothes.

I always play the princess.

I stole my Mammy's make-up.

I secretly have baths with My Little Ponies.

I don't have any friends that are boys.

I wore tights under my school uniform.

MICHELLE: Who can find a virtuous woman? For she is far more precious than rubies.

YASMIN: I'm sat waiting for you again, for what feels like hours and hours

And I don't think you're coming.

I tried to learn it all

Facts and places and languages

You always seemed strange to me

And I liked that about you

TAMIR:	*Sh'ma Yisra'eil Adonai Eloheinu Adonai echad.*
–	**Repeat**
TAMIR:	*Sh'ma Yisra'eil Adonai Eloheinu Adonai echad.*
–	**Repeat**
TAMIR:	*Sh'ma Yisra'eil Adonai Eloheinu Adonai echad.*

MICHELLE:	She does him good, not evil, all the days of her life.
BARRY:	Five

I'm the youngest of eight children, three girls and five boys. Mammy cuts all of our hair short. Bowl-around-the-head kind of job, to keep things easy

Daddy is the Del Boy of our small country town

He's in a business meeting in our kitchen

And I'm in my sister Brenda's Communion dress.

–	**It's a good product.**
–	**Oh I don't disagree.**
–	**It will do very well**

39

	(Telephone ringing noise.)
–	

BARRY:	Hello, Fitzgeralds.
	Daddy, it's for you. Are you in?
	I'm sorry he's in a meeting.
	I'll pass on the message. Thanks. *(Puts phone down.)*

–	**Who's this then?**
–	**This is. Mary.**
–	**Hello Mary.**
BARRY:	I'm not Mary.
–	**That's a lovely dress.**
BARRY:	I'm Barry.
–	**Out you go then, Mary**
BARRY:	I'm not Mary.
–	**We're in a meeting.**
BARRY:	It's me, Daddy. It's Barry.
–	**Run along then, Mary.**

MICHELLE:	Charm is deceptive, beauty is fleeting but a woman who fears the Lord will be praised
TAMIR:	*Sh'ma Yisra'eil Adonai Eloheinu Adonai echad.*
–	**Repeat**
TAMIR:	*Sh'ma Yisra'eil Adonai Eloheinu Adonai echad.*
–	**Repeat**
TAMIR:	*Sh'ma Yisra'eil Adonai Eloheinu Adonai echad.*
MICHELLE:	Femi, come back here. Let me see you.
	First comes the laughter, then the lecture
	You look like 80s Boy George. Kilode?
	I don't understand you, why do you do this? How will you find a husband? Is this how you will go to church? Why can't you dress normal ehn? Look at all your cousins – they're married. I don't get it, Femi. I only have one son but it's like you don't want to be my daughter…
YASMIN:	You always wanted a boy
	I know I'm not quite what you asked for

But you know I want to be just like you

And you don't mind that I try to dress
like you

TAMIR: Thirteen

It's my Bar Mitzvah. I'm in Jerusalem.

I've spent months practising my prayer.
The rabbi asking me to

\-   **Repeat**

Repeat

Repeat

TAMIR: And repeat until the words sink into my
body. Until the words inhabit me.

I stand in front of the crowd and I begin to
speak

Sh'ma Yisra'eil

Sh'ma Yis

Adonai

The words that are meant to take me from
boy to man aren't coming and I stumble

I fail

BARRY: I asked my mother if she was real.

               I don't have any friends.

               I let Colm's leg touch mine in the back of
               the van.

               I dreamt we held each other in the dark.

               I liked how it felt

               I like how it feels

TAMIR: It's the end of the celebration and sweets are
               being thrown into the air for the children.
               For a moment I forget my failed rite of
               passage and I run to catch them

–   **You're a man now, you are responsible
               for your actions, you should not eat
               sweets as a child does**

TAMIR: But these are my favourite

–   **You must drink whiskey to celebrate
               instead, a man should drink whiskey**

TAMIR: But I'm thirteen

–   **Le Chaim**

TAMIR: Le Chaim

TAMIR drinks the whiskey and squirms.

MICHELLE: I always thought, the Lord said we should
             come as we are…

YASMIN: When did you begin to learn anything that
             made me?

             When was I meant to become a woman?

             Because this in-between

             This middle doesn't make you proud

IT'S OKAY TO CRY

EMILY performs 'It's Okay to Cry' by Sophie, backed by BARRY on the piano and ELIJAH on drums. It is tender and vulnerable, almost like a letter to her younger self.

TIMELINE 4

17

YASMIN: **Wear a wedding dress in *Fiddler on the Roof***

9

MICHELLE: **Check out my first bum when shopping with Mum**

                12

3

BARRY: Having a bath in the kitchen sink

TAMIR: But you have the body of a man

26

JOSH-SUSAN: Susan is born

8

24

YASMIN: I'm having an affair with my manager
                 in the call centre

20   21

3   9

PUNCTUATE

–   Sorry I think you've

–   Yes

–   Oh

–   Got the wrong

- **asterisk**

- **hyphen**

- **asterisk**

- **hyphen**

- **asterisk**

- **hyphen**

- **asterisk hyphen asterisk hyphen
  asterisk hyphen**

- **asterisk hyphen**

- **asterisk hyphen**

- **asterisk hyphen**

- **question mark**

- **asterisk asterisk asterisk asterisk asterisk**

- **hyphen**

- Are we there yet?

- Are you there yet?

–	The destination has changed
–	The destination has changed

ELIJAH: I don't have the energy to take up space.

I don't have the energy to fill each compartment of 'he'. I need to be gas or liquid to reach each crevice, each hard corner, each arrogance.

I can dress up hard, stronger, grow this flesh harder, impenetrable – but penetrate me when I'm like that but not when I'm not, not now. Don't tell me you want it I don't want to hear it.

Solid is far from how I feel at the centre of things. Shifting, a form that comes together then apart, collapses and re-forms. A creature, an animal, some otherness. HE fits but there's that context there, always attached, a footnote. HE ASTERIX SEE APPENDIX ONE.

It is HE, I am that, but I will always shrink to fit. I will not spread my knees on the tube I will not talk louder than everyone else in the bar for no reason, I will cry, I will cry in public, I will paint my nails, I will be the me I always needed to be.

–	1. A medical diagnosis of gender dysphoria
–	2. A report from a medical professional detailing any medical treatment
–	3. Proof of having lived for at least two years in their acquired gender through, for example, bank statements, payslips and a passport
–	4. A statutory declaration that they intend to live in the acquired gender until death
–	5. If married, the consent of their spouse
–	Please can we talk about the toilet situation?
–	6. Payment of a fee of £140 (or proof of low income for reduction/removal of the fee)
–	7. Submission of this documentation to a panel, which the applicant does not meet in person

BARRY: I'm Cis.
But Sissy.
And for the longest time that sissy was in hiding. Or hidden.
I found myself so firmly fixed around my sexuality – a good gay schooled in a kind of silence. Suppressing those sissy signs and systems at play in my body.

But the camber of my construction screamed sibilant sounds.

It said – I'm going off script. I'm scrapping.
I'm sissifying. I'm sissiest.

Childhood memories are seen in a clearer,
truer light.

The flamingo flounce of my youth, which
scandalised and provoked new middle
names – gay, bender, poof – is finally
embraced. Albeit as a thirty-something
juvenile re-finding their femininity. I'm
looking outside myself.

I'm no coward.

I am strong.

It's not a loss of masculinity but my
volunteering to have it dismantled.

I'm Cis.
But Sissy.

–   Is this a cruising ground for gays, cos

–   dot dot dot

–   Kids in schools aren't safe in their toilets
        because

–   dot dot dot

–   Sexual predators pretending to be women
        and

–   dot dot dot

–   Stop filming me please, I

–   dot dot dot

–   If trans people can self-identify then

–   dot dot dot

–   You're in the wrong

–   dot dot dot

–   It's much cleaner in here

–   dot dot dot

–   I've never heard so many farts

–   dot dot dot

–   I just don't understand why

–   dot dot dot

–   Does it really matter that

–   dot dot dot

MICHELLE: She's waiting for me to take control. Be assertive. I'm waiting for her to let her guard down, be real with me for a moment. 'Cause I'm not the assertive type; even though I'm bossy, I'm no one's boss. But she wants me

to play the man for her. Take charge. Tell
her, 'come here'. But I can't…so I don't.
Then everything cracks and fizzles out.

I was just looking for some tenderness

–   It's my child

–   Yes

–   He hurts himself. He's depressed.

–   Is everything okay at home? At school?

–   Excuse me,

–   Excuse me,

–   Sorry

–   Excuse me, sorry

–   Excuse me, I think you might be in
            the wrong…

–   I think you might be in the wrong.

JOSH-SUSAN: Strip away label

               Slip inside skin

               Peel

Heal

Begin to feel

 –   Job

 –   Relationship

 –   The wrong country.

 –   Oi, you!

What?

This is…

Oi, you!

What?!

 –   Excuse me,

 –   Excuse me, I think

 –   Sorry,

 –   Excuse me, excuse me

 –   Sorry I think I might be in the wrong

 –   I might be in the wrong

 –   Body

 –   **Dimension**

-        Sorry, I'm in the wrong

-        **Place**

-        **Excuse me, sorry**

-        Excuse me, sorry, sorry, sorry

-        **I think you're in the wrong**

-        **seat**

-        **frame of mind**

-        **century**

-        **paradigm**

-        **hole?**

-        **conversation**

-        **uber**

-        Excuse me, excuse me

-        I think

-        I think

-        Sorry.

-        You're in the wrong.

53

–   sorry

–   excuse me

               excuse me,

               Excuse Me,

               Excuse Me,

               EXCUSE ME

               EXCUSE ME

               EXCUSE ME

YASMIN: Do you see me?

EMILY: They say we're born in the wrong body,
               and we're so desperate for acceptance we
               cling to any narrative that might help them
               understand. We didn't choose this, why
               would anyone choose this? What if I did?
               Would that make me any less real than
               you, less natural? Would I want to be? Fuck
               natural. Earthquakes are natural. Bedbugs
               are natural. There is no shame in getting rid
               of a gift you didn't ask for, or recycling it
               into something cooler.

54

This body is not a static thing but a journey
that isn't even close to being done, and if
I feel like it I will change course without
owing you any explanation.

It's like you're a sculptor. You take this thing
you've been given, this formless lump, and
start hacking away until something starts
to take shape. When you start out you may
tell yourself you won't go too far, that you'll
just chip away around the edges, polish
the surface a little. Maybe that is honestly
all you need. But maybe you get there and
realise there's so much more potential in this
thing. And then you will do whatever you
have to make it gleam.

–   Fashionable Brighton school has forty
        children who do not identify

–   Dot dot dot

–   Can you imagine

–   Question mark

–   I know someone

–   I know someone

–   I know

–   Exclamation mark

–   Their sex at birth

55

–	How would you know?
–	And another thirty-six are genderfluid
–	How would you know?
–	How can you know?
–	I know someone
–	I know someone
–	Interruption

MICHELLE: Anybody will do.
As in
any body.
I count the weeks in between
Last being touched
Name it 'the drought'
Text old lovers to enquire if
They miss my taste
Enough to come back
Or more realistically –
let's catch up soon x
I've done this before.
I've learnt being desired and loved are not
synonymous things.
I've substituted kissing for litre bottles of
water and I'm still not drinking enough.
I repeat the mantra, 'It's hard because it's
hard, not because you're flawed.'
But I've run out of lies to tell myself.
My throat is Saharan sand. And
My crushes never message back.

They move on to hobbies I am not privy to
or with women
Who never look like me.

–	Dash
–	Separate statements.
–	Know someone who transitioned and then transitioned back.
–	I mean make your mind up
–	Sudden outcry
–	I saw online
–	Add emphasis
–	I saw online
–	Read this thing
–	Semicolon
–	Between the clauses
–	It had to be Brighton didn't it
–	Question mark
–	Someone told me
–	Direct

- Someone told me

- Bold

- This rapid rise will at last force

- Interruption

- the government to step in when they do

- I hope there is someone there to pick up the pieces

- Emphasis

- Pick up the pieces

- Sudden outcry

- There's a school full of kids

- Where is that statistic from?

- Over half of girls who identify as boys have been victimised by sexual predators

- Maybe something is going on in Brighton

- Over half the signatures

- Sudden outcry

- I remember most of the signatures were from Brighton

- This is frightening

–	Bold
–	This is frightening
–	Emphasis
–	Who is looking out for the kids?
–	It's basically grooming
–	Underline
–	Just shows the state of times really
–	A self-fulfilling prophecy of a false market
ALL:	**BRACE**

PLASTIC COUTURE

EMILY and ELIJAH form a riot grrrl punk band. The lyrics are tabloid headlines around gender and trans issues.

TAMIR runs against a large sheet of thick plastic, using its sheen to apply lipstick and then write across it. They are wearing high heels, stockings and suspenders, black knickers, pearl necklaces and a fur coat. They struggle against the weight of the plastic until they finally break free of it. TAMIR wears the plastic like a fabulous couture gown.

MAX

YASMIN: So this is Max.

Walks on stage holding a photograph of their younger self.

If you can see, this is a picture of me when I was ten years old.

I know I look quite young. When I was little my mum was actually called into school because I was the shortest kid in my class by a lot. They calculated that I wouldn't grow much more than four feet. The same with my sister.

I also have short hair, and a *Wallace and Gromit* T-shirt. If you can see there.

Hands the picture to a member of the audience

My mum divorced my dad and we moved to a new house and when I went to play with the other boys on my street I told them my name was Max.

Max played football and wore baseball caps. Boys would knock on my front door and ask if Max was coming out to play and my mum would reluctantly call up the stairs for 'Max'.

It came to a bitter end.

Mark Derbyshire who was my neighbour found out I was actually a girl because his mum asked my new dad Kevin.

The boys on my street were so convinced that they forced me to show the oldest boy on the street my underwear behind the bushes. I did, and they finally believed I was a girl.

I look at this picture sometimes and think, even as a child, a very short child, maybe I knew more about how I wanted to be seen than I do now.

In fact, maybe I have just spent the last seventeen years moving slowly back to Max.

GRID 3

The grid is even messier now, as though all the gender-rule-breaking throughout the play has ruptured it. The actors break free of the grid – they throw costumes across the stage, glitter cannons go off, there is dancing, vogueing and Silly String. Lots of Silly String.

STORIES/JOKES

ELIJAH: When you're acting in a play and the director says can we just try that transition again, you say

            'Again?!'

YASMIN: I went to Victorian Day dressed as a chimney sweep

TAMIR: First time I gave a blowjob was behind Bournemouth Tourist Information Centre

BARRY: When I was younger, I was really into candlemaking.

MICHELLE: I was the first to grow boobs in my year and
              I didn't know what they were. So I used to
              flash them at my cousins thinking they
              were pecs.

ELIJAH: Does anyone have a power song? *(Waits
              for response.)* Ironically, mine is 'Dangerous
              Woman' by Ariana Grande.

EMILY: So a lot of potential partners are confused
              by the prospect of dating a woman with
              a dick, but I mean think of it financially –
              'You'll never have to spend money on strap-
              ons again!' I'm just kidding, I'm way too
              traumatised by this thing to put it anywhere.

JOSH-SUSAN: A woman dragged her child away from me
              the other day cos I was wearing a dress. I
              thought bitch what's your child going to
              catch…style?

YASMIN: I went to a Disney party when I was ten
              dressed as Prince Eric from *The Little
              Mermaid*, the other parents were so offended
              that when my mum picked me up she said,
              'We will just have to stick to animals from
              now on.'

TAMIR: I used to hate my facial hair so much that I
              dreamed about peeling skin off my jaw.

EMILY: Any sex reassignment surgeons in the house
              tonight? Call me.

ELIJAH: I saw a birthday card that said, 'Happy
              birthday brother, you're like a sister to me'

BARRY:	At thirteen, my main hobby was rollerblading aggressively through the town while listening to Alanis Morrisette's 'Jagged Little Pill'.
JOSH-SUSAN:	Sex in high heels is great – there's no punchline. Just advertising
YASMIN:	When I was younger, I had no friends
MICHELLE:	A year after I played the lead in my church play, I was hanging with two friends and we got talking about how good it was. One of them said, 'Ah the lead guy was sick – I wonder what happened to him?'
JOSH-SUSAN:	My acting career started with me winning the dying cowboy competition at Butlins Margate.
EMILY:	Does anyone here have a coming out story they want to share? *(If someone does, ask them for it.)* Okay here's mine. I took a dodgy legal high, had a panic attack and thought: 'Okay I need to tell everyone I'm a girl before I die.' I don't know what the optimal way to come out is but that's not it.
BARRY:	When I first started going to pubs in my home town, I used to have a little ritual. I would stand on the back steps, say a little prayer, push the door open and everyone would shout 'faggot'.

MICHELLE:	When I was seven, my younger brother decided that instead of having a bath, he would run downstairs naked and pee on me while I watched cartoons.
TAMIR:	I once drank so many double Americanos I thought I was having a heart attack and called 999.
YASMIN:	I asked my mum why she let me dress as a boy for so long and she said darling we were just happy to be alive
ELIJAH:	When I was a kid, I used to take off my shorts and pants and straddle the toilet trying to pee like a boy. I also used to tug on…
EMILY:	I often feel very watched. But right now I feel really seen. So thanks, for seeing me.

I KNOW A PLACE

The cast all sing – karaoke-style – to MUNA's 'I Know A Place'.

It is a big celebration of who they are, where they have been and where they (and all of the audience) are going.

The cast invite the audience to join them on the stage, and if they accept, the whole theatre becomes a dance floor.

End.

WWW.OBERONBOOKS.COM

9 781786 827296